My Favourite

Stories about Children

My Favourite

Stories about Children

Selwyn Hughes

My Favourite Stories about Children
compiled by Selwyn Hughes

Copyright © Selwyn Hughes 2001
ISBN 1-85345-194-0

All Scripture quotations in this publication are taken from the
Holy Bible, New International Version (NIV). Copyright ©
1973, 1978, 1984, International Bible Society. Used by permis-
sion.

This book is an edited compilation of quotes, anecdotes and stories collected by Selwyn Hughes during his 50 years in Christian
ministry. Whilst every reasonable effort has been made to trace
copyright holders, the publishers would be pleased to hear from
any not acknowledged here. With special thanks to ACP
Publishing Pty. Limited, Australia, from *The Australian Women's
Weekly*. Gervase Phinn, UK, from *Classroom Creatures*.
Christianity Today International, USA, from *Today's Christian
Woman*.

Concept development, editing, design and production by CWR.
Cover image: Photodisc. Internal images: Eyewire.

Printed by Cox & Wyman

Published by CWR, Waverley Abbey House, Waverley Lane,
Farnham, Surrey, GU9 8EP

Contents

Introduction

What was it that drew children to Jesus and He to them? Was it their ability to trust? ... to take risks? ... their curiosity? ... the things they say? It must have been all those things and more. Children are a gift from God (Psalm 127) and their contribution to life is something we ought to cherish.

Enjoy this little book of stories and quotes. And remember, every one of us is a child at heart.

Selwyn Hughes

The author's royalties from this book will be donated to a selection of Children's charities throughout the world.

CHILDREN ...
*Things They
Say in Church ...*

The answer to EVERYTHING

A pastor asked his Sunday School class one day, "What is white, has big ears and is fluffy all over?"

A little boy replied, "It sounds like a rabbit to me, but I suppose the answer must be Jesus."

Free INDEED

As the church organ played during the collection a child's voice was over-heard whispering, "You don't have to pay for me Daddy. I'm under five."

A
BUGGING
Question

"Please, Miss", a little boy asked his Sunday School teacher as she paused in telling the story of Lot, fleeing from the destruction of Sodom, "you said God told Lot to take his wife and flea out of the city – so what happened to the flea?"

CLEANLINESS
is next to Godliness

"Wash your hands! Wash your hands!" said a little boy angrily to his mother as she met him after Sunday school. "That's all we hear about here – germs and Jesus – and you can't see either one of them!"

Knock and the Door WILL OPEN

"Can we see Jesus with our eyes?", asked the Sunday School teacher.

"No we can't, because he is invisible," came a reply from a small boy.

"Well," said the teacher, "if He is invisible, how do we know He is there?"

"He's the one who opens the door for us at the supermarket."

Forever FUN

"What does Jesus promise us?" a Sunday School teacher asked her class.

"Ever-laughing life," a little girl responded cheerily.

GRANDMOTHER
of God

"Tell me what happened in your class today," said a mother to her little girl, following her first ever visit to Sunday School.

"We had Jesus' grandmother taking our class," she said.

"What do you mean?" asked the puzzled mother.

"All this lady did was tell us stories about Jesus and show us pictures of him."

HOP *to it!*

"What do you think of," said a pastor to a group of children in his Sunday morning children's talk, "when I say the word 'frog'?"

"God", responded one of boys at the front.

"Why is that?" asked the pastor.

"Because we don't come to church to talk about frogs," said the little boy.

Spiritual WARFARE

A little boy came running out of Sunday School shouting, "Where is he? Where is he? Let me at him."

"Where is who dear?" asked his mother.

"The devil," replied the boy. "Where is the devil? Today we were told to fight the devil and now I'm looking for him. So, where is he?"

Dog's LIFE

A little boy was asked by his Sunday School teacher why he was so unhappy.

"My dog has died," he replied, as tears fell from his face.

"Don't worry," said the teacher, "when you get to heaven the dog will be there waiting for you."

The little boy looked somewhat nonplussed for a moment, then asked, "Whatever would God want with a dead dog?"

Good QUESTION

"Always remember that we are here to help others," said the Sunday School teacher.

A puzzled little girl put up her hand and asked, "Please Miss, so what are the others here for?"

Heaven CENT

The Minister, talking in his Sunday sermon about heaven, said, "There is no money in heaven."

A little boy turned to his father and whispered, "Dad, then we must be in heaven!"

Book of LIFE

A Sunday School teacher asked her class: "If Jesus walked into this room right now, what would you do?"

One little girl thought about it and replied: "I would walk up behind Him, tap Him on the shoulder and when He turned round, I would smile, give him a Bible and say, 'This is your life!'"

Plane TALK

A group of Sunday School children were asked by their teacher to draw a picture of the Christmas story.

One little girl drew a picture of an aeroplane. When asked what it represented she replied: "That is the Flight into Egypt, Miss."

"And who is this supposed to be?" asked the teacher, pointing to what looked like a figure in the cockpit. "That", said the little girl, "is Pontius, the Pilot."

By
THE BOOK

Returning from Sunday School one summer day, a little girl asked her parents if they could stop at the library. When asked why, she explained, "This morning my teacher told me that the only way we get to heaven is if our name is written in the Lamb's Book of Life. I just want to make sure that my name is in there!"

Parental Guidance RECOMMENDED

One Sunday morning, close to Christmas, a pastor gathered all the children in the congregation around him to tell the story of Christ's birth.

When he asked if anyone knew the name of Jesus' earthly father, the children fell silent. The thoughtful silence was broken by one youngster eagerly calling out, "Virge!" Seeing their confused faces, he explained, "You know, Virge 'n' Mary!"

The WRITE *Stuff*

While sitting next to her daughter during the Sunday morning worship service, a mother noticed her child look down at the open Bible in her lap. In a low whisper, the little girl asked, "Did God really write all that Mummy?"

"Yes He did", her mother quietly whispered back.

Looking down at the Bible again, she said in amazement, "Wow! He has really neat handwriting."

Gems
OVERHEARD IN SUNDAY SCHOOL

"In the Bible Noah's wife was called Joan of Ark."

"Lot's wife was a pillar of salt by day but a ball of fire by night."

"Esau was a man who wrote fables and sold his copyright for a mess of pottage."

"The Israelites made a golden calf because they didn't have enough gold to make a cow."

"Salome was a wicked woman who wore very few clothes and she took them off when she danced in front of Harrods."

"Jesus was born because Mary had an immaculate contraption."

"When they arrived they found Jesus in the manager."

"In the Gospel of Luke they named Him enamel."

"A Christian can have only one wife – this is called monotony."

BIBLE *Class*

Reverend Bright, our vicar,
Came in our class today.
He started with a little talk,
Then we closed our eyes to pray.
He talked about the Bible,
And the prophet Abraham,
How God created everything
And how the world began.
Then he asked us all some questions
About the prophets and the kings,
David and Goliath,
And lots of other things.
"In a very famous garden
Grew an apple on a tree,
And who ate that forbidden fruit?"
And a voice said: "Wasn't me!"

God is ...

When I was little I thought God
was like *Captain Birdseye
– without the fish fingers.
I thought that God always smiled and
had a friendly face.
That He was tall and kind
and never shouted.

Now I am older I think that God
is like an old man with many children.
I think God has a sad and tired face
and He cries and groans
to see the world He made.

* An aged fisherman character used in
advertising for a brand of frozen food.

Letters to GOD

Dear God,
In school they told us about all the things You do. Who does it all when You are on your vacation?

Jane

Dear God,
Are you really invisible, or is that just a clever trick?

Lucy

Dear God,
Is it true my father won't get in Heaven if he uses bad words in the house?

Anita

Dear God,
Did you mean for the giraffe to look like that, or was it an accident?

Norma

Dear God,
Instead of letting people die and having to make new ones, why don't You just keep the ones You have now?

Jane

Dear God,
Who draws the lines around the countries?

Nan

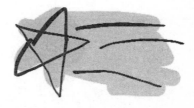

Dear God,
I went to this wedding and they kissed
right in church. Is that okay?

Neil

Dear God,
How come You are a jealous God? I
thought you had everything.

Jane

Dear God,
Did You really mean "do unto others as
they do unto you"? Because if You did,
then I'm going to fix my brother!

Darla

Dear God,
Thank You for the baby brother, but what I prayed for was a puppy.

> *Joyce*

Dear God,
I would like to live 900 years like the guy in the Bible.

> *Love, Chris*

Dear God,
Why is Sunday school on Sunday? I thought it was supposed to be our day of rest too.

> *Tom L*

Dear God,

It rained for our whole vacation and my father is really mad! He said some things about You that people are not supposed to say, but I hope You will not hurt him. He didn't mean it.

> *Your friend (but I am not going to tell you who I am)*

Dear God,

Please send me a pony.

I never asked for anything before. You can look it up.

> *Bruce*

Dear God,
Maybe Cain and Abel would not have killed each other if they had been given their own rooms. It works with me and my brother.

    Larry

Dear God,
I want to be just like my Daddy but not with so much hair all over my body.

    Sam

Dear God,
I bet it is very hard for You to love all of everybody in the whole world. There are only four people in our family and I can never do it.

    Nan

Dear God,
If you watch me in church on Sunday,
I'll show You my new shoes.
    Mickey D

Dear God,
We read Thomas Edison made light. But
in school they said You did it. So I bet
he stole Your idea.
    Sincerely,
    Donna

CHILDREN ...
Things They Say at School ...

Oh CRUMBS!

A little girl was found crying and distressed outside her classroom by the visiting School Inspector.

"What's wrong, little girl?" asked the inspector.

"Boo hoo!" she sobbed, "I want a big stick. Everyone else has got a big stick. But I haven't got one. I should have a big stick too!"

The Inspector was puzzled, until a teacher came along and explained, "She means biscuit. She wants a biscuit."

Charity begins WITH LOANS

A young boy asked his mother if she would let him borrow some money to take to school the next day so he could buy 65 roses.

Somewhat confused, the mother telephoned her son's school to ask for an explanation. The matter was quickly resolved when the boy's teacher explained that the children had been asked to contribute money for the treatment of cystic fibrosis.

Whispers of WISDOM

A little girl, born with a cleft palate, was embarrassed that she didn't look and talked like the rest of the children in her class. When asked about her lip, she would just say it was the result of an accident.

One day, a school nurse, giving her a hearing test, whispered in her ear, "I wish you were my little girl". From that day she was changed.

God has been whispering the same thing in our ears since the days of Eden.

Thirst for LIFE

A teacher was telling his class how Jesus changed the water into wine at the wedding feast of Cana. "What does this story teach us?" he asked a small boy.

"When you run out of wine," he ventured, "get down on your knees and pray."

Confidence TRICK

A little boy was asked by his aunt why he was chosen to represent his school in a quiz game.

"Because I am the smartest boy in the class," he answered.

"Did your teacher tell you that?" enquired his aunt.

"No", said the child, "I noticed it all by myself."

Stating the OBVIOUS

A little boy fell and bruised his leg as he came out of school.

One of the teachers rushed to his aid. Taking out her mobile phone, she said, "Tell me your name and number and I'll phone your mother."

"There's no need to tell my mother my name or my number," he said, "she knows both already."

Doing TIME

Just before he entered school for the first time a little boy asked, "How long do I have to stay in school Mum?" "Until you are about sixteen," she answered.

The little boy's eyes filled with tears as he said, "You won't forget to come back for me when I am sixteen then, will you?"

Teacher's PESTS

A rather unpopular school teacher who was off ill was sent a "Get well soon" card by her students. The message read, "Your class wishes you a speedy recovery, by a vote of 13 to 12."

Once Upon a Time – INTERRUPTED

"Once upon a time children, long, long ago, there lived a ..."

"Big, ugly monster Miss?"

"No David, not a big, ugly monster – a beautiful princess, called Imelda. She had eyes as bright and as green as sparkling emeralds. She had hair which fell down her back like a golden water-fall. Her skin was as white ..."

"As a ghost's Miss?"

"No, not a ghost's David; as white as the snow which covered the fields. Her lips were as red as ..."

"Blood, Miss?"

"No, not blood David; as red as cherries. But Princess Imelda was lonely. How she longed for a friend. As the seasons passed she stared from the high window in her castle. Then one day ..."

"Did she fall out Miss?"

"No, she didn't fall out David. She saw in the distance a great cloud of smoke."

"A fire-breathing dragon had come to eat her up."

"David, will you listen? It wasn't a dragon. It was a prince, on a great white horse. As he rode over the bridge ..."

"Did he fall off Miss?"

"No!"

"Miss, was there a wicked troll under the bridge?"

"David! Would you be quiet? There are other children in the class who might want to say something or ask a question. Now give somebody else a chance. Yes Amy, have you got a question to ask me?"

"Yes Miss."

"What is it dear?"

"May I go to the toilet please?"

Silent WITNESS

A teacher had briefly left her class one day and, on returning, found all the children sitting in perfect silence with their arms folded. She was so surprised at the unexpected silence that she asked for an explanation.

A little girl spoke out, "Miss, you told us that if you ever returned to the classroom to find all of us sitting perfectly quiet we would see you drop dead of shock."

Mind Your MANNERS

The first day of school, a little boy came home saying, "We can't use 'thank you' in the bathroom." "What do you mean?" his mother asked.

"There's a sign on the bathroom door outside my class", he explained, "It says, 'Please do not use – thank you.'"

Taken For A RIDE

An elementary school was having a problem with students who would not stop throwing rocks. The principal announced over the intercom one day that any student caught in the act would be taken home by him, personally.

Later that day, during recess, a teacher admonished a kindergarten pupil for throwing a rock. "Didn't you hear what the principal said?" the teacher asked in disbelief. "Yeah," replied the lad with some excitement, "That means I get to go home in the principal's car!"

Christmas Presents for MISS

Chocolates in a fancy box –
For the teacher who is tops!

A towel and an oven glove –
From Gemma Thompson with my love.

A bottle stands in thick brown paper –
All the best – from Darren Baker.

Perfumed soap from Lee and Chris,
You're our favourite teacher Miss.

Flowers in a coloured pot –

Happy Christmas, Helen Bott.
A china dog with painted face –
For the teacher who is ace!

And from the nuisance of the class
The Nativity encased in glass.
I know this year I've been a pain,
I'm sorry Miss – with love from Wayne.

And though she's taught for many years,
The teacher's eyes still fill with tears,
For children know the ones who care
And that is why those gifts are there.

A Christmas Story – INTERRUPTED

"It was a cold winter night when Mary and Joseph arrived in Bethlehem. Joseph walked ahead holding up his lamp to light the way."

"Didn't he have a torch Miss?"

"No, Briony he didn't have a flash-light. There were no torches in those days. I'll continue ... Mary was on the old donkey which walked oh so slowly. I think he knew that he was carrying a precious cargo."

"Miss I went on a donkey this year at Blackpool. It ran off along the sands

and my dad had to chase it. It kicked my dad and tried to bite him Miss."

"Yes, well this donkey was a very gentle donkey."

"Did it have bells on Miss?"

"No it didn't have bells on Briony."

"The donkey I went on at Blackpool had bells on."

"Right, well this one didn't. Now, Mary knew she was going to have her baby very soon. She felt very tired."

"Miss my dad was tired after he chased the donkey."

"Mary was tired because she had been travelling all day and was expecting a baby any moment."

"Miss, my Auntie Christine felt tired

when she was having my cousin Oliver.
She had swollen ankles as well and a bad
back and Miss she was always being sick.
She said it was the last baby she was going
to have because ..."

"Briony, just listen dear. Mary and
Joseph had been waiting such a long
time for the arrival of their very special
baby."

"Was it induced Miss. My cousin
Oliver was induced."

"No, Mary's baby wasn't induced
Briony."

"Miss what does induced mean?"

"I'll tell you when you're older
David. Joseph looked everywhere for
somewhere to stay. But there was no

room. There was only the stable where the ox and the ass slept."

"Miss what's an ass?"

"It's a donkey Briony."

"I wouldn't like to sleep with a donkey, Miss. The one in Blackpool was really smelly and tried to kick my dad and bite his hand."

"Briony dear, this was a very nice donkey in the stable."

"And did that one have bells on Miss?"

"No it didn't have bells on either. Soon Mary would have her very special baby and lay him wrapped in swaddling clothes in a manger."

"The donkeys in Blackpool were

mangy Miss – Dad said so."

"I said manger Briony not mangy. The Angel had told Mary not to fear. He had brought tidings of great joy but he told Joseph to take Mary and the baby and flee to Egypt."

"Miss, the donkeys in Blackpool had fleas Miss. My Auntie Christine was scratching the whole holiday and ..."

"Briony dear, I think we have all heard quite enough about the donkeys in Blackpool. Now just sit still and listen. And don't scratch. Yes, David what is it dear ...?"

Infant
INTERROGATION

(A child's conversation with a new
school teacher)

Infant: What's that?

Teacher: What?

Infant: That on your face.

Teacher: It's a moustache.

Infant: What does it do?

Teacher: It doesn't do anything.

Infant: Oh.

Teacher: It just sits there on my lip.

Infant: Does it go up your nose?

Teacher: No.

Infant: Could I stroke it?

Teacher: No.

Infant: Is it alive?

Teacher: No, it's not alive.

Infant: Can I have one?

Teacher: No, little girls don't have moustaches.

Infant: Why?

Teacher: Well, they just don't.

Infant: Can I have one when I grow up?

Teacher: No, ladies don't have moustaches either.

Infant: Well my grannie's got one!

CHILDREN ...
Things They Say in Prayer

The NAME of the Father

"God has many names," said the Sunday School teacher to her class one morning. "Jehovah – the Almighty One. Do you know any more?"

"Harold," called out an eager child.

"Harold?" questioned the boy's puzzled teacher.

"Yes, Miss. The Lord's Prayer says 'Our Father, who art in heaven, Harold be thy name.'"

POWER
in the Name

A little boy, who was struggling to peddle his bike out of a muddy furrow, was heard repeating over and over again, "In the name of Jesus, move! In the name of Jesus, move!"

An URGENT Prayer Request

One Sunday morning a little boy was becoming restless during a church meeting. When his father gave him some art materials to keep him busy he took one of the crayons and aimed it at an elderly woman five rows in front.

As the crayon hit her head she turned round sharply to see what had happened. The father, incensed at his son's action stood up, threw the boy over his shoulder and proceeded up the aisle to take the boy out of the church. As they went, the little boy yelled at the congregation, "Please pray for me!"

A–Z
of Prayer

A little girl was overheard saying the letters of the alphabet as she knelt down to pray at her bedside.

"Why are you doing that?" asked her astonished mother.

"I don't know what to pray for, so I say the alphabet and then God can put everything together the way He wants to."

Nothing TODAY, *Thank You*

"Do you pray every day?" asked a vicar of a little boy.

"No, Vicar," he said, "because there are some days when I don't want anything."

Made in
HEAVEN

"What does the Bible say about marriage?" asked the Sunday School teacher of her class.

One little boy gave it some thought, then replied, "Father, forgive them for they know not what they do."

Prayers @ Bedtime

A mother had been teaching her three-year-old daughter the Lord's Prayer. For several evenings, before she went to sleep, she repeated it after her mother. Her mother listened with pride as she enunciated every word, right up to the end of the prayer.

One night, however, she was ready to go solo: "Lead us not into temptation," she prayed, "but deliver us from e-mail. Amen."

BLESS
this Mess

A five-year-old offered the following prayer during family devotions one night; "Dear Jesus, sorry for the mess we made in the garden today." After a slight pause, he concluded, "Thank You for the fun we had doing it."

CHILDREN ...
Things They Say to Others

GONE *Fishing*

A child, seeing his beloved goldfish floating on the water, called his father to see if he could help. The father pronounced the pet dead and suggested they have a small funeral in the garden, then they could go to the ice cream parlour to mourn their loss.

Whilst the father searched for a matchbox coffin the boy saw the goldfish move. His father realised he had been mistaken as it was now clearly very much alive. Suddenly it dawned on the son that the ice cream was no longer justified. He was deep in thought for a moment before proposing, "Let's kill it."

HIDING
Your Age

A small child, seeing her great-grandmother for the first time, asked her age. The great-grandmother, not wanting to share her secret with the girl, said she could not remember exactly how old she was.

"Oh, I can tell you how to find out, Grandma," offered the child, helpfully. "Just look inside your underwear. Mine says 'aged 3–4 years.'"

Wet BEHIND *the Ears*

The following story is told by former Archbishop of Canterbury, Donald Coggan. It concerns a conversation with his little granddaughter:

"Grandad," she said, "were you on the Ark during the Flood?"

"No, my dear," the grandfather replied "I wasn't."

The grandchild, with a rather puzzled expression, asked, "Then how come you didn't get washed away with the others?"

FOREVER
Young

"Grandma," whispered a seven-year-old to her grandmother sitting beside her at the Christmas Eve Nativity play, "why doesn't baby Jesus ever get older? I've been to lots of these and he never seems to get any bigger."

WISE
Words

A small boy was pleased to have been chosen to play a key role in his school Nativity play, was asked by his mother which of the three wise men he would be playing.

"I bring gold," he said, "and my friend Frank brings sense."

Family
SUPPORT

A Pastor was asked by his little daughter, "Daddy, why do you always pray before you speak at church?"

"I pray," he said, "so that God will help me preach a good sermon that will bless people."

"Then why doesn't God ever answer your prayers?" she asked.

LOVE
Thy Neighbour

A seven-year-old bridesmaid was asked by a wedding guest if she would get married when she grew up. "Yes," said the little girl, "I am going to marry the boy next door."

"Oh," said the guest, "how can you be so sure?"

"Because I'm not allowed to cross the road."

My Father's
CHILD

A little girl, when asked her name, would always reply, "I am Mr John Jones' daughter." Her mother corrected her, saying, "Always answer by giving your name – Jane Jones.

"Aren't you John Jones's daughter?" asked the pastor soon after, in Sunday school. "I always thought I was" said Jane, "but my mother says I'm not."

Food for
THOUGHT

As she was preparing dinner the day before Easter, a mother tried to distract her hungry four-year-old son by explaining the importance of this holy day. She told him that because of what Jesus did, we could all go to heaven. "When will we come back to earth?" he asked. "We won't – we'll live there forever," she replied. "Then how are we going to eat dinner?" he shrieked.

Head in the CLOUDS

A little girl was anxious during her first plane flight. "What if the aeroplane falls down?" she kept asking, nervously. During take-off she squeezed her mother's hand so hard that her knuckles turned white.

However, once they were above the clouds, she released her grip and announced, "It's okay now. We're above the clouds – right next to heaven."

MIND
Game

While visiting his grandma one day, a four-year-old searched for his favourite board game. He found all the other game pieces, but couldn't find the marbles. Dismayed, he ran up to his mother with the news, "Grandma's lost her marbles!"

WHAT'S UP, *Doc?*

A four-year-old went to the doctor's office with a fever. The doctor looked in her ears and said, "Who's in there? Donald Duck?" She said, "No." He looked in her nose and said, "Who's in there? Is it Mickey Mouse?" Again she said, "No."

He put his stethoscope on her heart and said, "So who's in there? Could it be Winnie the Pooh?" "No", she replied, "Jesus is in my heart. Winnie is on my underwear."

Heartburn

One day, a little girl came up to her mother and said, "Mum, I know that Jesus lives inside my heart. But how do I tell him I love Him? Do you think if I write 'I love You" on a piece of paper and eat it, He'll get the note?"

Home TRUTHS

One day, a mother was explaining to her five-year-old daughter that if she chose to be disobedient, she would have to live with the consequences. "Oh, Mummy!" she exclaimed, looking terrified, "Please don't make me live with the Consequences. I want to stay here with you!"

These Shoes Were Made for WALKING

One day a mother asked her two-year-old daughter where her slippers were. "Downstairs in the kitchen," she replied. "What are they doing there?" her mother asked. "Nothing," she replied. "They can't walk because they don't have feet in them right now."

Heads UP

Watching TV together one night, a three-year-old was sitting on the sofa while his grandfather sat on the floor in front of him. Observing the top of his grandfather's head, the little boy anxiously exclaimed "Grandpa, your head is sticking out of your hair!"

All EARS

One day a three-year-old girl was playing with her toys. Her mother, who was folding laundry across the room, noticed her daughter's shirt was dirty and needed to be changed. After calling her twice with no response, her mother yelled, "Did you hear me young lady?" The little girl answered, "Yes, Mama. My ears heard you, but my legs didn't."

POWER *Nap*

During a recent visit to her grandparents, a two-year-old was sitting at the kitchen table eating her lunch. Her grandmother joined her, closed her eyes, and bowed her head to say a silent prayer for her food.

The little girl watched inquisitively and, as her grandmother raised her head and opened her eyes, asked, "Nana, did you have a nice nap?"

Heaven on EARTH

Two young brothers walked together behind their parents as they left the town carnival after a wonderful day out. One was overheard telling his younger sibling, "This is what heaven is like – except it's all free!"

Helping HAND

A three-year-old accidentally spilled his juice on the floor one day. Deciding to clean up the mess himself, he dashed to the back porch to get the mop.

Suddenly, realising it was dark outside, he became apprehensive about reaching out of the door.

His mother reminded him that Jesus is everywhere – even in the dark. The little boy thought for a minute. Then, putting his face to the door, he said, "Hey, Jesus, if you're out there, will you hand me the mop?"

Ageing
BEAUTIFULLY

While sitting on her grandmother's lap, a three-year-old leaned back and said seriously, "Nanna, do you know you have lots and lots of wrinkles on your neck?" Then, after a pause she continued, "But they make a really nice pattern."

On REFLECTION

A lady was standing with her grandson in a large department store, waiting to be served. A young shop assistant came past pushing a full-length mirror on rollers. She stopped for a moment, flicked her hair away from her face, then continued on her way.

The grandson, fascinated, asked, "Nanna, why doesn't that lady just have a little mirror in her bag like you do to check your hair and make-up?"

On the BOTTLE

A three-year-old girl heard her mother tell someone one day that her eight-week-old son had colic. Asked later how her brother was, she replied, "He's alcoholic."

Up for DEBATE

After moving from Britain to Hong Kong a father reported that his three-year-old had difficulty adjusting to many aspects of his new culture. But one aspect he took to quickly was haggling. When discussion about bedtime came up, he would say, "Mum, Dad, let's make a deal."

The EYES
Have Had It

"I'm not tired," said a six-year-old, rubbing her eyes. "It's just that my eyes don't want to open right now."

ICE WEATHER
We're Having

Startled by a heavy hailstorm, a four-year-old rushed to a window to see what all the noise was. Seconds later, he sprinted into his parents room, yelling, "Look, look outside. It's raining ice cubes."

Shared EMOTIONS

Two young brothers were fighting one day, observed from a distance by their aunt. "I really hate you sometimes!" the elder boy was heard to shout, to which the younger retorted with dignity, "Yeah? Well the feeling is neutral."

DRESS *Code*

"Where has Mummy gone?" asked a three-year-old girl, as her mother disappeared into the office of a local business. "She's gone to get a name and address for your Daddy," replied her sister. Looking puzzled, the small girl replied, "But our Daddy doesn't wear a dress."

MIXED *Invitation*

A nine-year-old girl had just attended her first school disco. Asked how it went, she replied, "It was dreadful! The teachers wanted us to dance with the boys."

RESISTIBLE *Offer*

As she waited at a friend's house for her to return from an errand, a visitor was pleased when the young son of the house came into the room to keep her company.

After trying to think of something to say, he asked whether or not she had eaten. Delighted at his manners, she said thank you, but she had eaten earlier. "Well if you are still hungry," he went on, persuasively, "I think there are cold sausages and a slice of stale bread."

A Teenager's Letter of DESPERATION

Dear Mum

I hate to write to you this way but you've got to know.

I know you think I have been seeing too much of Dave lately, and that you believe he's too old for me and all that, but, like I told you, we really love each other and want to be together all the time. He was really great when I told him I was having his baby and he said that decided it, and I should just leave school and be with him and he would look after both of us forever.

So I won't be coming back home. We've found a flat and though it is tiny and a bit damp, it is really cool and I know we are going to be just fine. Dave's got a new job with more money, and that means I won't have to get a job but can just stay at home and prepare for the baby.

We're not living that far away but I'm not going to give you our address because you would only come after us and try to make me come home, but I promise I will keep in touch and when the baby is born we will bring him to see you.

Somehow I am just sure it's going to be a boy and that's great, because

Dave wants to teach him to play football. But a girl would be really cool too. So, Mum, try not to worry. I'm in good hands and I know Dave really loves me and will look after us both.

I just want to say that I love you and I am sorry that I've hurt you and Dad, but I hope you can try to be happy for us.

With very much love,
Debbie

P.S.

Not a word of this is true. The fact is, I've failed all my college exams and I just wanted you to get things in perspective.

CHILDREN ...
*Things the Bible
Says About Them*

Proverbs 20:11

Even a child is known by his actions, by whether his conduct is pure and right.

Proverbs 22:6

Train a child in the way he should go, and when he is old he will not turn from it.

Jeremiah 1:7–8

But the Lord said to me, "Do not say, 'I am only a child.' You must go to everyone I send you to and say whatever I command you. Do not be afraid of them, for I am with you and will rescue you," declares the Lord.

Psalm 34:11

Come, my children, listen to me; I will teach you the fear of the Lord.

Matthew 18:3–6

And he said: "I tell you the truth, unless you change and become like little children, you will never enter the kingdom of heaven. Therefore, whoever humbles himself like this child is the greatest in the kingdom of heaven. And whoever welcomes a little child like this in my name welcomes me. But if anyone causes one of these little ones who believe in me to sin, it would be better for him to have a large millstone hung around his neck and to be drowned in the depths of the sea."

Mark 9:36–37

He took a little child and had him stand among them. Taking him in his arms, he said to them, "Whoever welcomes one of these little children in my name welcomes me; and whoever welcomes me does not welcome me but the one who sent me."

Mark 10:13–16

People were bringing little children to Jesus to have him touch them, but the disciples rebuked them. When Jesus saw this, he was indignant. He said to them, "Let the little children come to me, and do not hinder them, for the kingdom of God belongs to such as these. I tell you the truth, anyone who will not receive the kingdom of God like a little child will never enter it." And he took the children in his arms, put his hands on them and blessed them.

Isaiah 66:13

As a mother comforts her child, so will I comfort you ...

1 Thessalonians 2:7

... but we were gentle among you, like a mother caring for her little children.

NATIONAL DISTRIBUTORS

UK: (AND COUNTRIES NOT LISTED BELOW)
CWR, PO Box 230, Farnham, Surrey GU9 8EP.
Tel: (01252) 784710 Outside UK (44) 1252 784710

AUSTRALIA: CMC Australasia, PO Box 519, Belmont, Victoria
3216. Tel: (03) 5241 3288

CANADA: CMC Distribution Ltd, PO Box 7000, Niagara on the
Lake, Ontario L0S 1J0. Tel: (0800) 325 1297

GHANA: Challenge Enterprises of Ghana, PO Box 5723, Accra.
Tel: (021) 222437/223249 Fax: (021) 226227

HONG KONG: Cross Communications Ltd, 1/F, 562A Nathan
Road, Kowloon. Tel: 2780 1188 Fax: 2770 6229

INDIA: Crystal Communications, 10-3-18/4/1, East Marredpally,
Secunderabad – 500 026. Tel/Fax: (040) 7732801

KENYA: Keswick Bookshop, PO Box 10242, Nairobi.
Tel: (02) 331692/226047

MALAYSIA: Salvation Book Centre (M) Sdn Bhd,
23 Jalan SS 2/64, 47300 Petaling Jaya, Selangor.
Tel: (03) 78766411/78766797 Fax: (03) 78757066/78756360

NEW ZEALAND: CMC New Zealand Ltd, Private Bag, 17910
Green Lane, Auckland. Tel: (09) 5249393 Fax: (09) 5222137

NIGERIA: FBFM, Helen Baugh House, 96 St Finbarr's College Road, Akoka, Lagos. Tel: (01) 7747429/4700218/825775/827264

PHILIPPINES: OMF Literature Inc, 776 Boni Avenue, Mandaluyong City. Tel: (02) 531 2183 Fax: (02) 531 1960

REPUBLIC OF IRELAND: Scripture Union, 40 Talbot Street, Dublin 1. Tel: (01) 8363764

SINGAPORE: Campus Crusade Asia Ltd, 315 Outram Road, 06-08 Tan Boon Liat Building, Singapore 169074. Tel: (065) 222 3640

SOUTH AFRICA: Struik Christian Books, 80 MacKenzie Street, PO Box 1144, Cape Town 8000. Tel: (021) 462 4360 Fax: (021) 461 3612

SRI LANKA: Christombu Books, 27 Hospital Street, Colombo 1. Tel: (01) 433142/328909

TANZANIA: CLC Christian Book Centre, PO Box 1384, Mkwepu Street, Dar es Salaam. Tel: (051) 2119439

UGANDA: New Day Bookshop, PO Box 2021, Kampala. Tel: (041) 255377

ZIMBABWE: Word of Life Books, Shop 4, Memorial Building, 35 S Machel Avenue, Harare. Tel: (04) 781305 Fax: (04) 774739

For e-mail addresses, visit the CWR web site: www.cwr.org.uk

Other titles in this series include:

My Favourite Prayers

A thoughtful collection of prayers of petition and praise concerned with all aspects of the Christian life. An inspiring gift for new Christians as well as for those experienced in the faith.

My Favourite Quotes and Anecdotes

An amusing book of stories that work as well at the dinner table or party as they do in the pulpit or the boardroom. A great gift for young and old alike and a helpful aid to anyone involved in public speaking.

Tails

Devotonal Activity Books: £3.95
Story Books: £4.95

Tails is an exciting series created to help young children understand the Bible. The books are written by the award winning children's author, **Karyn Henley**, and the characters are created by **Debbie Smith** who works with the Oscar winning **Wallace and Gromit**™ team.

Devotional Activity Books
Bible Friends

Learn about great Bible friendships such as Jonathan and David and Mary and Martha.

Who is Jesus?

Discover the One who is the Son of God, the Prince of Peace, the Friend and Helper.

Let's Worship

Learn to worship anytime and anywhere, alone or with others.

Story Books
Friends Forever

No matter how many mistakes we make true friends always love us.

Who's Whoo-oo-oo?

Jesus is revealed as our best Friend.

Twigs and the Treasure Box

Tails friends discover the greatest treasure of all.

**One-Year
devotionals**

This attractive series features easy to read selections from Selwyn Hughes' most popular work, **Every Day with Jesus**. The luxurious presentation of these pocket-sized books makes them an inspired gift or travel companion.

Meeting with God

Living with Jesus

Walking in the Spirit

Pocket Encouragers
£3.99

This new series offers biblical help, guidance and encouragement. Each title explores various aspects of the Christian experience, such as relationships, Bible study and coping with responsibility. Some content is common to all titles, with unique material that relates especially to men, women, leaders or young adults. Great gifts!

Pocket Encourager for Men

Pocket Encourager for Women

Pocket Encourager for Leaders

Pocket Encourager for Young Adults